WAR OF WORDS

The funniest Neil Warnock quotes!

by Gordon Law

Copyright © 2018 by Gordon Law

No part of this publication may be reproduced, stored in a retrieval system or transmitted in any form by any means, electronic, mechanical, photocopying, or otherwise, without prior written permission of the publisher Gordon Law.

gordonlawauthor@yahoo.com

Printed in Europe and the USA
ISBN: 9781729331200
Imprint: Independently published

Photo courtesy of: Ramzi Musallam

Contents

Introduction..4

Can You Manage?...7

Best of Enemies...25

Off the Pitch...41

Managing Players..55

Call the Manager..63

Fan Banter..83

A Funny Old Game...89

Ref Justice..107

Introduction

Neil Warnock is one of the most colourful, controversial and successful managers in the English game.

An experienced tactician, Warnock continues to conjure up the most unlikely of accomplishments through expert man-management and ensuring tireless effort from his players.

He is the only manager to lead four different clubs to the top division following his exploits with Cardiff City, which was also a record eighth promotion.

But the veteran boss has such a focused pursuit of victory that he has no qualms about clashing with literally anyone who stands in his way.

Throughout his nomadic career, Warnock has had entertaining war of words with managers such as Rafa Benitez, Gary Megson and Stan Ternent, while players such as El-Hadji Diouf, Joey Barton and Carlos Tevez have felt his ire.

Like a true Yorkshireman, Warnock speaks his mind and his rants at referees are always comical after decisions have gone against him, while his blunt honesty is refreshing to hear.

When captured by TV documentary cameras, the old school manager's half-time rollickings made hilarious viewing and revelling as football's panto villain, the abuse and banter with opposition fans brings great merriment.

His harsh put-downs, amusing observations and enjoyable anecdotes make Warnock one of football's most engaging characters and I hope you enjoy this unique collection of his quotes.

Gordon Law

WAR OF WORDS

CAN YOU MANAGE?

WAR OF WORDS

"I'll always fight my corner, say what I want. Sometimes it gets you in trouble but that's what Yorkshire people are like."
Neil Warnock is honest as ever

"I can't replicate how I feel when that whistle goes on nights like that, knowing you've won it, that people are going home smiling. You don't get that sat on my tractor in Plymouth or doing the shop in Tesco."
After Cardiff's late win over Wolves

"I'll tell you when he's had enough, not that computer."
He knows when a player is tired

Can You Manage?

"You might say, 'Eh, he's a big mouth', but you've got to be passionate, haven't you? If you aren't, you very often don't win. I think if you're successful you haven't got that many friends, have you? You don't really want them, either. Look at Sir Alex [Ferguson]. Dearie me. He isn't bothered about friends, is he?"

Warnock takes a leaf out of Sir Alex's book

"It's time for a new, moderate Mr Warnock. At the moment there will be no teacups thrown around the dressing room. That might change in the closing weeks of the campaign, mind you."

The Sheffield United boss vows to take a calmer approach on managing

WAR OF WORDS

"The good thing about these early kick-offs is that you can go out for a meal and still be all in your pyjamas for half eight."

Warnock likes his early nights

"I've ordered some suits made out of the finest Italian cloth! Wearing a suit might help calm me down a bit and not go as mad."

The Blades manager aims to get rid of his tracksuit after winning promotion

"It's not for me to tell [Fabio] Capello his job. Otherwise, I'd probably have got him to the World Cup final."

The Leeds boss rates himself highly

Can You Manage?

"When I'm doing an ingrown toenail operation, I find my patient talking to me and I'm not listening. At the end I say, 'I'm very sorry, Mrs Kirk, I was away – I was just picking the side for Saturday'."

Warnock worked as a part-time chiropodist while managing Scarborough

"It probably hasn't quite sunk in yet. I daren't have a drink, I'd probably be drunk in five minutes... I have to say, the biggest plus for me is having three weeks extra of holiday. I'm cream crackered at the minute."

After sealing promotion to the Premier League with Cardiff

WAR OF WORDS

"I was looking to Arsene and said, 'Look at the dugouts Arsene, they're miles away, you won't hear me today!' And he looked nonchalantly and said, 'Neil, you will find a way!'."

The Blades manager on his 1,000th game at the Emirates Stadium

"I was picking the eggs from the chickens and feeding the ducks and I'm on my tractor but there was something missing. It's like a poison."

On missing football when he took a break

"At my age, I should be at the seaside on a deckchair."

The 69-year-old is enjoying it at Cardiff

Can You Manage?

"We'd had a great run in the FA Cup, Burton Albion, so the TV cameras came up and we did a story. I still had my surgery then… so I put my white coat on and got my scalpel out. We got one of the lads up on the table and I said, 'This lad, he's had a problem with his feet for a number of weeks'. So they started filming, right. Now I'm not saying the guy was thick, but the player had on a pair of monkey feet, I was taking the p*ss, and this guy just filmed it – hair everywhere and six claws. And he put it in! They showed it on telly."

The qualified chiropodist on a TV prank

"I'd like this to be my last club."

Just how many times has he said this?

WAR OF WORDS

"I was a northern lad and I thought going beyond Watford was the end of the world in those days."
Warnock on why he rejected the Chelsea job

"As long as they play well, I'm sure managers don't care what they wear. I'm surprised at Christmas time that we haven't got a pair of boots with flashing lights!"
He has a new concept for football boots

"I once went to an interview at Norwich and they asked if their fans would accept the 'Warnock Way'? I said what do you mean, winning? I don't understand what the 'Warnock Way' is, me."
Responding to taunts about his playing style

Can You Manage?

"I tell my children they must have good manners. I'm okay except between five to three and 10 to five during a game. Then somebody else takes over."

The QPR manager becomes his alter-ego when he is in the dugout

"As a manager at any level, when things are going wrong it's with you every minute of the day. You go home and your wife will be talking but you are not listening. You are thinking, 'Do I pick him, or him?' You'll watch TV but you aren't really watching, you're doing it to be sociable. Inside you are thinking, 'How do I leave a top player out?'"

Warnock always has football on his mind

WAR OF WORDS

"When I saw Barbra Streisand yell back at a heckler, I thought, 'At least it's not just me that gets angry at work'."

Warnock sees comparisons with the singer

"For me to get the Manager of the Month award, I'd have to win nine games out of eight."

The Sheffield Utd boss at his ironic best

"I don't get many managers wanting to have a drink with me. There's a few, but I keep their identities quiet in case it damages their reputations."

Warnock on his footballing counterparts

Can You Manage?

"I know I was seventh choice but that don't bother me. It's a great club and it's nice to be able to put something back into it."
Warnock loves being the underdog after re-joining Crystal Palace in 2014

"This is the first time in my career I've had money to spend and I'm going to enjoy every single minute. I am in Utopia. This man is like a dream come true."
The QPR boss just can't believe his luck!

"It bugs me when I see other managers getting top jobs and I know they're not as good as me."
He has a high opinion of himself

WAR OF WORDS

"I've had my phone on ever since Jose's departure, but I guess Roman [Abramovich] must have misplaced my number."
Jobless Warnock is waiting for the call

"When the chips are down, the top dogs usually come up smelling of roses."
After QPR's unbeaten start to the season

"It's seven years today, my anniversary [as manager], and it was my birthday yesterday, so it's been a great weekend for me. I'd better be careful with the missus otherwise I'll probably put her in the club."
He celebrates seven years at United

Can You Manage?

"I know I'm out of work, but that's a bit over the top, isn't it?"

He saw his wife cutting a '10 per cent off' voucher from a breakfast cereal packet shortly before getting the Palace job

"We lost to both cup winners last year, and you can't do more than that."

Well, you can Neil

"I don't think Jose Mourinho is a better manager than me – he's just had more opportunities. He's a top manager, but I think I am too."

The Blades boss rates himself highly

WAR OF WORDS

"Sharon was a wreck, crying her eyes out. I thought at first she was re-watching the last episode of Downton Abbey."
His wife's reaction after the QPR sacking

Q: "Do you regret the fact that today's results have taken Plymouth Argyle out of the play-off positions with only weeks remaining of the season?"
A: "Son, I don't give a f*ck."
The Argyle boss' response to a journalist

"We have had a couple of players in on trial who have been frankly embarrassing."
The manager just says it how it is

Can You Manage?

"I used the Olympics in my team talk. When I went to bed, Kelly Holmes turned me on – which is sad for me isn't it? But when I watched Kelly and the relay lads, their ambition was to aim for the top. Now I think I have a group of lads who should look at themselves and also aim for the top."

On guiding the Blades to victory over Leeds

"We did have time for some sight-seeing, wandering round the square and through the souks. We saw all the snake-charmers with their cobras. I was a bit disappointed no one offered to swap [my wife] Sharon for a camel."

Warnock takes in the sights on a scouting trip to Morocco for QPR

WAR OF WORDS

"I'm not a communicator by tweet, I'm afraid, so I was always going to be the last to know."

He feels Twitter influenced his QPR sacking

"We had to shop at the other end but who's to say Aldi is not as good as Waitrose. I like going in Aldi, they've got a nice bottle of whisky in there."

The Cardiff boss compares his budget to big-spending Wolves

"I didn't want to frighten myself!"

The Blades manager refuses to watch Chelsea's win over Blackburn and takes in a nature documentary instead

Can You Manage?

"Well if the person think it's funny then so be it – I'm not against anything that makes people laugh. I'm all for that. And I've certainly been called a lot worse."

He isn't fussed about his nickname 'Colin W*nker' – an anagram of Neil Warnock

"More comebacks than Sinatra. I can't let the game go."

Warnock just cannot retire from football

"It's been the easiest week of training. We've just been chasing shadows to get used to it."

He jokes about preparations for Cardiff's daunting cup tie against Man City

WAR OF WORDS

BEST OF ENEMIES

WAR OF WORDS

"For many years I have thought he was the gutter type – I was going to call him a sewer rat, but that might be insulting to sewer rats. He's the lowest of the low and I can't see him being at Blackburn much longer."

Former Blackburn striker El-Hadji Diouf angers Warnock after abusing QPR's Jamie Mackie as he lay on the floor in pain with a broken leg

"The two managers I really dislike are Stan Ternent and Gary Megson. The old saying that I wouldn't p*ss on them if they were on fire applies."

Warnock makes his feelings clear when talking about his rival managers

Best of Enemies

"I don't think Wally [Downes] was coherent. His eyes were bulging when he barged into me. I never normally see him before, after or during matches – I just hear him... Wally was trying to say I was telling people to break legs, which is absolute garbage."

The Blades boss was shoved by Reading coach Wally Downes which sparked a touchline melee after Downes apparently misinterpreted a Warnock gesture

"Because Forest are struggling and he's under pressure, Joe couldn't find anything about his team to talk about. Any comments Joe has to make about me are water off a duck's back."

Joe Kinnear had called him a "complete prat"

WAR OF WORDS

"He took his glasses off as well so he meant business. But it wasn't that bad – even the ref laughed when he came over. I told the fourth official to get him sent to stands, to get him away from me, I said 'Can you send him upstairs?'"

On assistant Kevin Blackwell squaring up to Forest coach David Weir

"They'll justify it. They'll get the police officers to say what they did. But the ordinary guy in the street, even the Derby fans think it's an absolute stitch-up."

After Cardiff's game at Derby was called off due to heavy snowfall which coincided with the Rams having several players injured

Best of Enemies

"I had always known Stan Ternent was a d*ckhead but when Sheffield United played Burnley in 2001 he behaved like a deranged lunatic. I'd told my assistant Kevin Blackwell to keep an eye on Ternent. I knew he'd be trying to put pressure on the ref. So when Ternent came round the corner, frothing at the mouth, Blackie told him to leave it out. That was all the encouragement Ternent needed. He launched himself at Blackie and butted him. Blackwell swung a right hook and smacked him on the nose. He sploshed him good and proper. In Ternent's autobiography he tells how he gave Blackwell a good hiding. But we saw the incident differently. Blackie had a little cut on his lip. Ternent was in bits."

Then-Burnley manager Stan Ternent had a touchline dust-up at Bramall Lane in 2001

WAR OF WORDS

"And then Carlos Tevez, football's equivalent of a murderer out on bail, scores the goal that kept West Ham up and put us down."

Warnock is still angry with the role the ex-West Ham forward played in Sheffield United's relegation

"There are two or three managers I just can't stand. I detest them. So far I've kept to myself what I hate about them. But what they say gets a lot of coverage. I'd love to come back and give my version. I'd like to tell everybody why I dislike these people."

I wonder if Gary Megson and Stan Ternent are on the list?

Best of Enemies

"What he said in the local paper was an absolute disgrace. I know he is only a young manager, but I don't think he should be saying things like, 'We have to make sure we win, whether we do it by aggression or intimidation'. That is almost inciting the crowd and I think that is out of order, personally. Like father, like son."

The Rotherham boss on his Bristol City counterpart Lee Johnson's pre-match comments. Warnock has had plenty of spats with his dad Gary

"The sooner he leaves the country the better."

Warnock lays into Carlos Tevez after he refused to warm up for Roberto Mancini

WAR OF WORDS

"I don't suppose Gary [Megson] will be wanting to have a pint with me afterwards... but then not many people do."
Warnock after the 'Battle of Bramall Lane'. The game was abandoned with West Brom leading 3-0 because Sheffield United had only six players left on the pitch

"It's been very difficult working with him [administrator Brendan Guilfoyle], he has a high opinion of himself. I found out that the agent he brought in received £100,000 within days of selling Victor Moses for £2m and I think I could have sold him in my sleep."
Fighting fires at cash-strapped Palace

Best of Enemies

"I won't deny that I flipped my fingers in his direction, but only because I was so disgusted and frustrated at being humiliated by a fellow manager. If the same circumstances arose I would do the same again. I held out my hand for six or seven seconds but he kept on talking and turned his back. There was no mix-up, he even looked me in the eyes."

Warnock gave a V-sign to Norwich manager Nigel Worthington after an away defeat

"Anyone who knows Gary Megson knows he is the biggest moaner around."

The manager is not Megson's biggest fan

WAR OF WORDS

"I hope he breaks his f*cking leg next time!"

The Sheffield United manager shouted to Leeds boss Kevin Blackwell after Gary Kelly's 50-50 challenge on Craig Short

"One young [Bristol City] yobbo caught me. I think one of the security guards trod on him as he fell to the floor because I heard him squeal. He needs his eyesight looking at because he was that close I don't know how he missed, he just grazed me. There's millions of people who would like to do that!"

The Palace boss after getting caught up in a pitch invasion at Ashton Gate

Best of Enemies

"I'd never heard of them but when you are a foreign manager like Rafa Benitez, you probably don't give two hoots about what Sheffield United think."

Rafa Benitez named a weakened side for Liverpool's game against Sheffield United's relegation rivals Fulham, which the Cottagers won. They also escaped relegation by one point at United's expense

"I hope Liverpool never win another trophy under Benitez. I like them as a club but I would be very pleased to see them win nothing."

Still sore about Benitez' actions a year later

WAR OF WORDS

"He wanted to know where I was. Sharon [Warnock's wife] told him I was doing a press conference and I'd be back soon. So Sean Bean started swearing at her and my five-year-old son. 'It's your f*cking husband that got us relegated, he's a f*cking w*nker'. That's Sean Bean, the tough guy actor. Some kind of tough guy, eh, reducing a five-year-old kid and his mum to tears."

Warnock on an incident involving Blades fan and actor Sean Bean after they were relegated from the Premier League in 2007

"He isn't English!"

When asked why Liverpool's Stephane Henchoz allegedly spat at him

Best of Enemies

"I think [Richard] Scudamore is an absolute disgrace. I'd love to get him in a room on my own for an hour no holds barred."

Warnock fumes at the Premier League chief executive over the Carlos Tevez affair

"You can f*ck off Pinocchio. Get back in your f*cking cupboard!"

The Blades boss yells at Liverpool coach Phil Thompson during a League Cup semi

"I hear Gary [Megson] is writing a book. That's good news for insomniacs everywhere."

The Blades boss on his rival

"I haven't thought about shaking hands yet. But I don't think I should get into that because the last time I heard from Rafa he was threatening to sue me if I mentioned [the row] again. It was an email and I think it was his solicitor who was threatening legal action but I think it had Rafa's name on it. I've got it in a scrapbook at home."

The Leeds manager is unsure if he'll get a frosty reception from Chelsea interim boss Rafa Benitez

"Charlton is the only place I can go and not be the number one most hated man if the chairman [Simon Jordan] turns up. I hope he is going."

On visiting the Valley with Palace

Best of Enemies

"It's not printable on Sky, I don't accept it at all. I think it's totally out of order. I think it was a total disgrace, I used strong words and I meant every word of them. He has got to learn in the British football game, you have manners, you have a bit of class when you have won a game and he has got to learn that, I am afraid."

The boss is riled by Wolves boss Nuno Espirito Santo after he celebrated a 1-0 win over Cardiff in exuberant fashion with his team before offering him a handshake

"I personally hope Mark Hughes follows me again and destroys another team of mine."

Warnock on departing Leeds blasts Hughes who replaced him at QPR

WAR OF WORDS

OFF THE PITCH

WAR OF WORDS

"I'd ask him to look at himself. He goes out to find a pool table in a Sheffield Wednesday pub the day after we'd beaten our bitter rivals at Hillsborough. Hello Alan – work it out for yourself, son. It doesn't seem to have been the brightest idea he's ever had, that's for sure."

Exasperated after Alan Quinn was arrested following an alleged bar fight

"It's up to the fans to help me now. If they see any member of my squad in a pub, club, bar, whatever, I want them to ring me up and tell me. If my players want to drink they can get p*ssed in the safety of their own homes."

Warnock wants Blades supporters to keep an eye out for him

"My big dislike is traffic jams and that's why I'm going to live in Cornwall when I retire. The only traffic jam there is when the tractor pulls up at the post office."

The manager hates getting stuck in the big city traffic

"Our promotion has brought a few journos out of the woodwork who seem to have a grudge against me, particularly Patrick Collins in The Mail on Sunday. I take Collins' columns to bed with me, I suffer from insomnia and find after a couple of his paragraphs I drop off for a good night's sleep."

The Hoops boss is not happy with the writer's article on him

WAR OF WORDS

"One of the lads, Shaun Derry, did not train Tuesday because he had a groin problem, so I was told by physio. So imagine my concern when I saw him on the dance floor breakdancing and doing the splits. As I was dancing with Sharon at the time I whispered to him, 'I suppose this means you are fit for Saturday?'"

Warnock on Palace's 2007 Christmas party

"All the restaurants were full and we couldn't get in, so we celebrated with a takeaway kebab instead."

On how Sheffield United celebrated their promotion

Off the Pitch

"My wife will be glad about [Jose] Mourinho coming to Bramall Lane because he's a good looking swine, isn't he?"

Warnock's wife Sharon is thrilled about United's promotion to the Premier League

"I am off to Cornwall to get on my tractor for a few days."

The manager will plough some fields after getting fired by QPR

"They don't have windows there, do they?"

He jokes with Steve McManaman who said he didn't feel the cold in the BT Sport studio because he was from Liverpool

WAR OF WORDS

"I started talking to him about this game. I said, 'Bloody hell, we've scored some good goals'. I shouted to him, 'We've had a bloody great time, what about you?' His head's gone up and he was looking at me and you could see him thinking, 'What the f*ck are you talking about?'. I got too carried away in the end, went too close and he backed away and disappeared into the bracken. You couldn't tell he was there any more. He must have thought I was a right nutter."

The QPR manager bumped into a stag during a bike ride around Richmond Park

Off the Pitch

"If we go up I'll even guarantee that I'll drown my players in champagne – non-vintage – to their hearts' content."

Sheffield United boss Warnock knows how to celebrate promotion

"I loved doing talkSPORT with Alan Brazil. He said to me one morning, 'When we finish, I'm going to nip down the road, are you coming?' I asked him, 'What are you going for?' For a couple of bottles of Champagne! It was 10 in the morning."

Boozy breakfasts while working on radio

WAR OF WORDS

"The trouble is that the players who cause these problems are thick, and they are not going to get their brains back, are they? That is for sure. Is Paddy all right, mentally? Not really, but we've known about that from the day he joined us. I wouldn't take issue with him being out at a curry house until three o'clock in the morning. There is nothing wrong with that, provided it is one of the nights I have said they can go out. He didn't have a dessert, anyway, so he must be watching his diet."

Goalkeeper Paddy Kenny had his eyebrow bitten off during a street fight in Halifax

Off the Pitch

"I can't drink any beer, lager, Guinness – I've never been able to. I don't think my dad drank it either, for whatever reason, so maybe it passed down to me. I'm more of a wine man, red or white. How much do I pay? Well I'll pay £5 or £6 for a good Shiraz in Tesco, or if it's a special occasion I'll treat myself to a new St George's, which is about £15 a bottle."

Warnock on his favourite tipple

Waitress: "Would you like sugar?"
Warnock: "You don't have sugar with a body like mine."

A common response from the Leeds United manager in restaurants

"Fortunately for me, I don't have that problem, I don't have hairs hardly anywhere. My daughter can't believe how smooth I am. I don't mind it, I don't shave very often, it must be very difficult for people who do. It leaves you open to all sorts of injuries."

Warnock was left perplexed after Marco Asensio was unavailable for Real Madrid after picking up an infection from shaving

"People say to me why don't I go on Twitter. Why would I want thousands of people sending me hate mail every week or wanting to know what time I dropped the dog off at the vet? It does my head in."

Warnock is not a fan of social media

Off the Pitch

"I once took Sheffield United all the way to China and we had an opportunity to go see the Great Wall of China. Two players out of 25 wanted to go see it. All the rest of them wanted to do was have their bloody earphones on and get their music pumped in. There's more to life."

The Leeds manager on the modern-day footballer

Friend of Warnock's wife: "I'm sorry, I don't know anything about football."
Warnock: "That's all right, you can be one of our directors."

A common quip when meeting non-football people

WAR OF WORDS

"I like period dramas and I cry at films a lot. I love watching The Way We Were [with Barbra Streisand and Robert Redford]. The kids love it when I'm slobbering away. I look through DVDs of films nowadays and they are all violence. No story in them. Sad really."
Warnock loves to watch a tear-jerker

"I have not enjoyed watching England for 20 years, I much prefer watching Coronation Street."
The Blades boss likes a bit of Corrie

"I'm sure the Queen would have invited me, we got on so well the last time we met."
On William and Kate's royal wedding

"I think her mother loves me because we're a similar age."

The QPR boss on his unlikely friendship with Delia Smith's mum

"I was playing marbles on the lawn with my eight-year-old son on the first day back at training this season. I normally have 200 things going through my mind but all I had to worry about was these marbles."

On being out of work during the summer

"My wife was hoping I'd get the sack so we could retire down to Cornwall with the children."

The Blades manager on retirement

WAR OF WORDS

MANAGING PLAYERS

WAR OF WORDS

"It's probably one of the most satisfying parts of the job. Forty-two grand for Paddy Kenny. I know he don't look the part, shape-wise. But keep feeding him burgers, eh? If he had a perfect shape he wouldn't just be the best goalkeeper in the Republic of Ireland but in this country."

Warnock hails his goalkeeper

"The first goal, one header from a header and the kid's through on goal. It's Raggy A*se Rovers. For the second one, when have you seen Clint Hill mess about like that? He thought he was Jose Enrique or someone."

Warnock fumes at Clint Hill for QPR's defeat against Millwall

Managing Players

"Leon [Cort] was a reluctant sale but we're a very nice team and the Championship is a tough league."

The Eagles boss sold the centre half because he rarely got booked

"I said if he played well he could have a few days off. He is shooting off to catch a train. I think he is going to France, I can't tell with him. He is a rogue."

The QPR manager on Adel Taarabt

"I tried to get a pen and write a 'For Sale' sign on him but he was too quick for me."

Warnock on Palace forward Shefki Kuqi

WAR OF WORDS

"I'll probably have had enough of him by Christmas, so hopefully he'll score 10 or 15 goals by then and get himself a move."

On managing QPR captain Adel Taarabt

"What I like about is, I love looking at him, he is such a happy man and he makes me feel good."

Palace midfielder Alassane N'Diaye makes Warnock happy

"[Shefki] Kuqi missed a good chance, it went to his head. He could have just controlled it, but that's Kuqi for you."

His blunt assessment on the Palace striker

Managing Players

"Shipps was that good he surprised me! It's almost like watching in black and white – he looks even older than me... I've told him I'm going to go right out and sign a better player than him in the January transfer window."

The Blades boss praises Neil Shipperley after he scored a brace against Burnley

"You could see I've got a lot of control over him cos I called him over and told him to calm down and then he nearly got booked twice in the next two minutes."

Warnock on trying to stop Palace striker Marouane Chamakh from getting a red card

"He has no responsibility whatsoever. The players aren't allowed to pass to him in our half. I told them that. I decided pre-season. He's liable to do something we haven't thought about."
On how he manages Adel Taarabt

"Tommy Johnson is brainless and talented, which suits our system perfectly."
Warnock on his Notts County striker

"I certainly don't agree when he says he didn't move for the money. Money is a big thing for Shefki [Kuqi]."
Warnock doesn't believe his striker

Managing Players

"You need someone to grab people by the throat – in a nice way – and get them going."
On signing Joey Barton for QPR

"He doesn't know what he's going to do next, so the full-back doesn't have a chance, does he?"
On Palace winger Yannick Bolasie's trickery

"I just thought he was a disgrace. I will fine him as much as I possibly can. I told him to his face, 'You've let me down and you've let the team down'."
The QPR manager is critical after Armand Traore's red card against Aston Villa

WAR OF WORDS

CALL THE MANAGER

WAR OF WORDS

"The way it has all come out so far, you would think I was guilty of committing more crimes than Osama Bin Laden."

The Sheffield United boss is accused of encouraging his players to feign injury in the 'Battle of Bramall Lane' against West Brom which is abandoned when only six United players are left on the pitch

"Charlton's players should be disgusted with themselves – if they'd put that effort in when [their manager] Alan Pardew was here they would not be in the position. They don't play Crystal Palace every week."

Palace's Warnock after being defeated by local rivals Charlton

"I hope we can rough him up. Needs must."
On his plans for Arsenal's Aaron Ramsey

"Twenty minutes from kick-off, with the lads about to come in from their warm-up, I was in the dressing room getting my thoughts ready when my phone went. I thought it must be someone important to ring me at this time. I answered and a guy said, 'Mr Warnock? It's Specsavers here. Your contact lenses have arrived, will you be picking them up?'"
The QPR manager did go to Specsavers!

"Does day follow night? I haven't a clue."
The Palace boss is baffled

WAR OF WORDS

"There's no way I would've trusted him with a penalty. You've got to have somebody a little bit more cool, and he's not like that, Jason. He can whack a 35-yard free-kick in here and there but a penalty, with all the pressure on him at a place like White Hart Lane – not in a million years for me. I think a centre-half might have done a bit better! Obviously, he never meant to put it up there."

Warnock as a pundit on Jason Puncheon's penalty which he blasted high and wide for Palace against Spurs

"If corner kicks hadn't been invented, this would have been a very close game."

The Blades boss after defeat at Newcastle

"I counted eight chances and they were all sitters. My five-year-old daughter would have scored three of them."

After Sheffield United edged a narrow win over Colchester in the FA Cup

"It was like I used to say when I was a manager up north, we looked like southern softies."

His Palace side wasn't tough enough

"You say cheats don't prosper but I think in this case he has done."

Warnock blames Bradley Johnson for Joey Barton's red card for QPR

WAR OF WORDS

"You know what [Kevin] Muscat's like, he wants to get a response. I'll tell you something, should I? Muscat will not get a booking or a sending off because he is too f*cking sly. He does it when nobody's looking. He's a sh*tter. So we don't retaliate, we f*cking play. He wants somebody to go out there and elbow him and get sent off. We don't do that, we just f*cking stick at it now."

Part of Warnock's Sheffield United team talk for a game at Millwall which was covered by a TV documentary

"I didn't expect him to score, but to be fair he's lethal from a yard isn't he?"

On Sol Bamba's match-winner for Cardiff

"Paddy has a balloon on his forehead like you have never seen. If somebody headbutted me like somebody has headbutted Kenny, then I would chin him."

Blades goalie Paddy Kenny had a tunnel bust-up with Millwall's Kevin Muscat

"Paddy McCarthy was breathing through his backside after two games in 48 hours."

On the Palace defender's breathing habit

"So, Arsenal you are favourites and odds on to win. Your balloon flies so high, but beware, we have a pin."

The Blades boss before the FA Cup semi

WAR OF WORDS

"Kevin Doyle will never get an easier hat-trick than that... it's a good job that they sold Ibrahima Sonko to Stoke otherwise they could have had 10. But if you defend like that you'll get beaten by Bodmin and Saltash – never mind a team like Reading."

After Palace's 4-2 defeat at Reading

"We've had quite a number [of incidents] since I've been at the club, people headbutting each other and all sorts. When you're living with someone for 10 months a year, which we do, that kind of thing's going to happen. It's like a marriage."

The Blades manager on loving relationships

"My missus, Sharon, could have tackled better than we did. And, boy, she doesn't half pack a good tackle."

The Blades boss gives too much information

"Their goals were just comedy. You'd probably win £250 on Candid Camera for that second one."

On Palace's defending against Forest

"I've gone on record as saying Real Madrid would struggle to look good against them."

The Sheffield United boss ahead of the FA Cup tie against... Walsall

WAR OF WORDS

"Harry Redknapp phoned me and said it's the 21st century – how long since we put a man on the moon? And yet FIFA won't let us have cameras on the goalposts?"

On Freddie Sears' 'ghost goal' at Bristol City

"Gary Johnson is supposed to be a gentleman – unlike myself – and he nodded straight away that it was a goal."

The Palace boss feels cheated by it

"We didn't make it easy for my age by missing two or three chances that my missus could have put in."

The boss after Cardiff's win over Barnsley

"Julian Speroni has been super, the challenge on him was a bit naughty. But if he was my player I would have told him to have gone in like that, I don't like goalkeepers!"

He doesn't mind goalies getting roughed up

"You only need to breathe on Andy [Johnson] for him to go down."

Warnock reckons the striker likes to dive

"It will be a cracking match and a close one – maybe decided by a referee's decision, an odd bounce or something like an over-the-line goal."

Warnock stating the bleeding obvious

WAR OF WORDS

Neil Warnock: "[Joleon] Lescott, who's got him? Why have you [Jagielka] got him?"

Phil Jagielka: "It all happened so quick in the middle..."

Chris Morgan: "It's just the way it happened."

Warnock: "F*cking just the way it happened. Listen, who do you have to pick up. Is it in f*cking black and white or what? Who do you pick up, you? Lescott! And we last f*cking two minutes! Can't you f*cking get him by the time he comes to take a f*cking kick? Can you not get to pick him up by the time he gets from there to there? Whoever's in the f*cking box."

Morgan: "There's f*cking three people at the back, yeah."

Warnock: "But is Lescott one of them?"

Morgan: "But Craddock and the f*cking two other big f*ckers. So what do I do?"

Warnock: "You pick Lescott. And if one of the others scores, I don't f*cking blame you! And you [to Phil Jagielka] pick your f*cking man up. If he's the spare man, I take the f*cking blame!"

Morgan: "It isn't in black and white gaffer, you pick up who ever is f*cking there!"

Warnock: "So Lescott's got nobody on him, has he?"

[Morgan smashes a water bottle into the dressing room floor]

An epic half-time rollicking by Warnock to Sheffield United's Chris Morgan and Phil Jagielka, which was captured by a TV documentary

WAR OF WORDS

"I am not happy we lost 4-0, but sometimes you have to smile through adversity."

QPR were thrashed by Bolton

"I don't think the lad would've had a free header with [Carl] Fletcher on the pitch but he had to rush off because his wife was having contractions. Women can be so inconvenient can't they? It's cost us a bloody point!"

Warnock is irked the Palace midfielder's wife went into labour

"I regretted not putting myself on the bench after 10 minutes of the game."

On his first match as Leeds manager

"I was delighted for Ifill. He was sharp and lively and deserved his goal. I just hope his missus fits in with us when she has their baby!"
Warnock hopes Sheffield United winger Paul Ifill's overdue first child does not arrive on a match day

"I think that's why they threw the last goal in, so they didn't go to Man City away. We heard the score."
Warnock is irate at the Palace stadium PA who told fans Man City could be their next opponents after a 7-0 win over Sheffield Wednesday while the Eagles' cup tie with Newcastle was ongoing. Palace then lost in extra time

WAR OF WORDS

"Not in the least! It was a lovely dance and I enjoyed every minute. All I did was jump up and down, run on the spot for a bit and then jump up and down again. I only wish I'd been able to throw in a handstand as well. Do I regret it? Do I hell. If I can't be happy after beating our local rivals then there's something wrong with the game."

He doesn't regret doing a war dance after the Blades beat Sheffield Wednesday away

"It would have taken a brave man not to wear brown pants after comparing our team sheet with theirs."

The Notts County boss after playing the might of Arsenal in 1991

"I told him to calm down a bit. To be fair he didn't do much – he was concerned about his lad who had blood coming out of his nose. If he wants me to speak for him I will do – I know everyone on the commission!"

Palace's Warnock after his QPR counterpart Paulo Sousa was sent to the stand

"It was a bad miss and it gets worse every time you look at it. And instead of going a goal up we lose by three, which could have been five. I've told Neil [Danns] to come up and tell you how he missed it. I'm not sure he will though."

The Palace boss after his midfielder fluffed a big chance

WAR OF WORDS

"We defended like fairies in the first half but the first two goals could have come straight out of the Premier League."

BBC Match of the Day bosses rule that the QPR manager's "fairies" comment was "unacceptable" after a viewer complained

"Somebody's just given me a video of the game. I don't know why they handed it to me because there's no way I'm going to watch that again."

Warnock won't torture himself anymore

"We couldn't pass water!"

The Eagles manager rages at his players

Call the Manager

"I brought my son tonight because he wanted to see [Emmanuel] Adebayor – I told him he wouldn't get a kick and I was right!"

After Palace's Carling Cup loss to Man City

"We can't get too downhearted about the result and cry ourselves to sleep. The lads were waiting for the teacups and I said, 'Well played' to them."

After the Blades were beaten 3-0 by Palace

"He usually whacks the pigeon off the top of the stand with those but the goalie had no chance."

On Aron Gunnarsson's strike against Forest

WAR OF WORDS

FAN BANTER

WAR OF WORDS

"Something has got to be done. The man could have been carrying a weapon. People might laugh, but you've only got to look at what happened to Monica Seles to see how things could end up."

A Gillingham fan confronted Warnock

"This lad came running onto the pitch and I told him he was an idiot for coming on but that he hadn't done any real harm. Then when we got over to the stands a police officer told him he was nicked. I just asked them to show a bit of common sense and leave things at that, then they told me I was as bad as he was!"

Just three weeks later, Warnock led a Blades fan back into the stand

Fan Banter

"I joke with their fans that, when I do pass away, I hope they all have a minute's applause for me at Ashton Gate and remember the good times I've given them. I don't want a minute's silence when I die... I'd like a full minute of chanting 'Warnock is a w*nker'."

His request to the Bristol City supporters

"I don't think I've ever been a banker. I think that's what they were calling me..."

Warnock on the Wolves fans' chants

"They're almost like Yorkshire people transferred to Wales."

On the Cardiff City supporters

"The fans chanted, 'Warnock, Warnock, what's the score?' and I signalled to say, '1-0, but there is plenty of time left'. The fourth official came up to me four minutes later and said the head of security has said 'If you incite the crowd any more you will be removed from the touchline'. They'd probably put me in prison in padlocks."

Bantering with the Leeds supporters

"We'll probably get more fans than if we'd signed Ronaldo."

The Bury boss acquired Indian international Baichung Bhutia in 1999 – 3,603 watched his first game

Fan Banter

"They said I'll take you to the directors box and I said, 'Are you joking? This is Reading. I'm not going anywhere near their fans'. I said I'll watch it on my phone but I couldn't get 3G in the dressing room. I ended up going in the TV section with a few of the guys and when we got the first goal they shot off. I saw the second goal and obviously celebrated running around the little room on my own."

The Cardiff manager after getting banished to the stands at Reading

"He didn't incite the crowd – we plan to report the 4,500 people who called him a fat b*stard."

After Paddy Kenny jubilantly celebrated the Blades' winner in front of Hull's fans

WAR OF WORDS

A FUNNY OLD GAME

WAR OF WORDS

"You wouldn't put your animals through that. It's ridiculous."

The Cardiff manager is angry his side have to play two days after the international break with many of his players flying back

"As long as the whole of my massive salary was paid within 28 days, then I would buy so many tosspots – although, come to think of it, their current squad would do – and f*ck 'em up so badly. Then I'd retire to Cornwall and spend the rest of my life laughing my f*cking head off."

When asked if he would manage Sheffield Wednesday

A Funny Old Game

"I had a one-night stand with a new bedtime partner this week. There are pictures too, but there is no need to get a super-injunction to keep it quiet. Sharon knew and she was very understanding. After we won the Championship on Monday I took the trophy home... So that night I asked Sharon, did she mind if I slept with it? I love her to bits, but it was only for one night. She slept in the spare room."

He spent time with the original Football League trophy after QPR won the title

"The Championship is a hard league and you're playing against different opposition every week."

The Leeds manager stating the obvious

WAR OF WORDS

"People say that me and Ian [Holloway] are very similar. Other than Ian being a lot uglier than me, we're both passionate, we both care about our teams and we've both done it the hard way."

The Palace manager on his contemporary

"We got on a bus and before we got to the hotel, the driver said he had a message from his boss that he wouldn't take us to the ground unless I paid for the bus. That's the last time I was at Newcastle. I haven't got my money back for that bus by the way!"

He recalls his last visit to St James' Park with Palace in 2010 after hearing the club had fallen into administration

A Funny Old Game

"My only asset was pace. I was very quick but I was brainless. At Rotherham they used to shout, 'Open the gate!' when I was going down the wings, but I'd run out of breath before I got there. I got my brains as a player when I was about 31, but by that point my legs had gone... Who was I most like? Ronaldinho, only without the skill."

Warnock on his time as a player

"The closest me and Cloughie have come is when he tried to kiss me after a testimonial match, but I smelled the aftershave and skipped past him."

The Notts County boss on Brian Clough

WAR OF WORDS

"We are going to get great Premiership football, end to end at 100mph, but you are not going to have a good international team even if Houdini is the manager."

He says England's poor form is due to the number of foreign players in the Premier League

"One of the press guys told me this morning that on [Damien] Delaney's Instagram he says he's agreed [to sign a new contract] so somebody at the club will tell me eventually. Unfortunately Damien can't tweet me but no doubt he'll let me know. It's good news if it is true."

On reports of a new deal for Palace defender Damien Delaney

A Funny Old Game

"Things are pretty tight at the moment. I've cut out the starter on my lunch at the training ground – I'm down to the main course and the dessert now!"

Warnock has to watch what he eats at cash-strapped Palace

"They must know somebody at the Football League, Norwich, getting their fixtures like they have. Poor old Dave Jones [former Cardiff City manager] was moaning about it the other day, I think Delia Smith must be cooking something for them."

The QPR boss reckons the Canaries have a favourable Championship run-in

WAR OF WORDS

"I once rang him up and was on for 10 minutes about players and he told me about every player, their strengths and their weaknesses. I put the phone down and I said 'I bet he even knows the Dunfermline groundsman'. So I rang him back and said 'Hey Alex, I forgot to ask you about the Dunfermline groundsman' and, by God, he did know his name and where he came from!"

The Blades boss on Sir Alex Ferguson

"If I had to pay to watch a team, it would be Arsenal. They're like a Rolls-Royce that you can't take your eye off. We're somewhere between a Ford Anglia and a BMW. You don't know what you'll get."

The Sheffield United manager goes car-azy

A Funny Old Game

"The sandwiches were fantastic today – all the lads made a comment because they didn't think they were going to get any!"

He is happy with Palace's grub despite the club's financial troubles

"We are not going to Everton looking for autographs, we are looking for points and that is the difference."

Ahead of the Blades' trip to Goodison Park

"He told me he wants to be in Europe within 18 months. Whether that means we're all going to Majorca next summer, I don't know."

On Palace chief Simon Jordan's ambitions

WAR OF WORDS

"If we are going to go Americanised, we are going to have all these girls waving things every time there is a goal. You ask them to run up and down in Sheffield with very little clothing on – it would be hard work for them."
He doesn't like the influx of glitz from the US

"When I first came to the club six-and-a-half years ago, the only chance we had of playing in Europe was taking on a team of waiters at the end of the season in Malaga."
Targeting European football for Sheff Utd

"I think it's the worst job in football."
Warnock doesn't want the England role

A Funny Old Game

"The fans should bring their boots, especially if they can play at the back. And my hip's feeling a bit better, so we'll see."

The boss on Palace's injury crisis

"I don't really know what a billionaire could do for Palace – I have only been here six weeks. You'd better ask the chairman. There are not a lot of billionaires in Yorkshire."

On reports a businessman was buying Palace

"If something has gone wrong, we say it. He is almost a Yorkshireman with a Portuguese accent."

The Blades manager on Jose Mourinho

WAR OF WORDS

"I think it is these stupid boots, they're like carpet slippers. Don't talk to me about these boots."

After DJ Campbell got injured in training

"I might buy some wine for when he comes, but I'll drink it myself."

Cardiff boss is looking forward to coming up against Pep Guardiola in the cup

"As a proud Yorkshireman, I'll be among the first to offer Leeds my commiserations. Well, I will as soon as I stop laughing."

The Blades boss on Leeds falling into the third tier... before he became their manager

A Funny Old Game

"I can't afford to keep giving my wife the same amount of money as the fine; it's a double whammy for me."

The Eagles boss had to pay £9,000 for his post-match comments against Chelsea

"I am looking forward to going back on talkSPORT and BT after [finishing as a manager], when you can say what you want and enjoy it."

After picking up an FA charge over what he said after the Blues game

"If we get a little bit complacent we know we're going to get our bottoms spanked."

A bum deal for the Palace manager

WAR OF WORDS

"I don't give two hoots about West Ham... it would be nice to be puffing on a cigar now but we don't do things like that."

After Sheffield United beat fellow strugglers West Ham 3-0

"When Crouch was first mentioned, I didn't think we could afford one of his shoe laces."

Warnock says Tottenham striker Peter Crouch is out of QPR's price range

"Matches don't come any bigger than FA Cup quarter-finals."

Warnock at Sheffield United. How about the semis?

A Funny Old Game

"You can love [Robbie] Savage or loathe him – a bit like me really. But he's done well to make a living with the ability he's got. He is long past his sell-by date."

Warnock on the Wales midfielder

"We've got three away games coming up where we cover 1,200 miles in just a few days. If we win all of them, I'll show my backside on Sheffield Town Hall steps."

On Palace's away fixture woes

"Sousa seems a nice fella and he's a smooth b*stard so my wife will like him."

He pays tribute to QPR boss Paulo Sousa

WAR OF WORDS

"I remember the day when they sold Brian Deane and Jan Aage Fjortoft. It was like when President Kennedy got shot – that's how deeply I felt."

Warnock on his love for Sheffield United

"A lot of people thought Simon [Jordan] and I would fall out within weeks. One of us is outspoken, demanding and doesn't suffer fools gladly, and the other is, well, just the same."

He has lots in common with the Palace chief

"I mean the Scots they can talk for England, can't they, the Scots."

Warnock as a TV pundit

A Funny Old Game

"I think Paul [Lambert] was embarrassed when he accepted it, to be honest. There was only one Manager of the Year in my eyes."

After the Norwich manager claimed the award, despite Warnock's Championship title win with QPR

"I think the new owners for City have been absolutely fantastic. We're trying to find one of these Sheikhs, wherever they are. We're hoping they come to the match and bring their family. Then hopefully a brother, a sister, an uncle or an auntie can take a fancy to us and put a bid in to Simon Jordan."

He says Palace need to find a rich owner

WAR OF WORDS

REF JUSTICE

WAR OF WORDS

"I shouldn't really say what I feel, but [Graham] Poll was their best midfielder in the move for the goal. You saw him coming off at half-time and at the end. He smiled so much, he obviously enjoyed that performance. I think the referee should be banned. We worked hard without the help of the ref. We lost in the semi-final of the Worthington Cup at Liverpool when their goalkeeper Chris Kirkland should have been sent off. The referee then was Alan Wiley, who was the fourth official here, and they love every minute of it."

Warnock fumes at referee Graham Poll (and Alan Wiley) after Sheffield United's FA Cup semi-final defeat to Arsenal

"I think the first [handball], the statistician's gave it down as a save, not handball... it's embarrassing, how that cannot be given as a penalty, he can't even say he's in a bad position."

He slams Michael Oliver after QPR had two penalty appeals against Alan Hutton denied

"I think the only chance we have of getting a penalty at the moment is somebody picking the ball up and throwing it at the referee. I said to the fourth official, 'How does it feel when you see you've made a mistake?'. He said, 'It hurts'. So there will be one or two people hurting tonight."

The Palace manager on not getting the rub of the green from the officials

"It's almost an assault. He [Craig Dawson] comes from two or three yards away and smashes him [Julian Speroni] in the face. I don't understand why at least one of the officials can't see that. I have not seen something like that since Bert Trautmann."

Referee Mark Clattenburg gets a blasting after Warnock had to substitute the groggy Palace keeper

"They have got to give the decision and then upset Sir Alex. I know people don't like upsetting Sir Alex but they have got to give what is there."

After Luton Shelton was denied a penalty in the Blades' loss against Man United

Ref Justice

"I didn't think it was a penalty. There was no contact. Apparently the ref has said there was intent, so that means there are going to be a lot of free-kicks given if there's intent but no contact. But I think Liverpool know they are fortunate because 95 per cent of people associated with the game would not have given a penalty. Unfortunately, one of the five per cent is wearing black and it was his decision, and we have to accept it. These things even themselves out – so they tell me – but it's not easy to digest."

After referee Rob Styles ruled that Blades defender Chris Morgan brought down Liverpool's Steven Gerrard

WAR OF WORDS

"David Elleray was that far away he would have needed binoculars. I really think it's about time we use the means to sort these things out rather than relying on some bald-headed bloke standing 50 yards away."

Warnock is angry at David Elleray after Sheffield United were knocked out of the FA Cup at Southampton

"I gave him 10 out of 10 after our Worthington Cup tie at Colchester this season and [Southampton boss] Glenn [Hoddle] will probably give him 10 this time. It means he'll average about five for the game."

Warnock continues his rant on Elleray

Ref Justice

"Why did the referee play four minutes 55 seconds of injury time and not the four minutes that was shown? You've got to ask him, he has refused to see me. They go back to their jobs, referees, and give no thought about professionals like us having to work as hard as we've done tonight. 'So what? It's only a penalty, it's only a goal, it's only an extra minute, I'm enjoying myself'. Dear me, it's disgraceful."

Bristol City scored after the minimum stoppage time of four minutes had been played to deny Palace victory

"Referees always have an answer, just so long as you give them enough time to think of one."

The Sheffield United boss just loves refs

WAR OF WORDS

"F*cking hell, what's the difference?! Lino, what's the f*cking difference?! We're away from home, that's the f*cking difference. We're in London. That's the f*cking difference. We're in London, aren't we?"

The Sheffield United boss, miked up for a TV documentary, screams at the linesman after one of his players is booked

"Steve Bennett knows the rules but not the game. Until referees get a Neil Warnock educating them at their weekly get-togethers, these things will keep happening."

Warnock, who is a qualified referee, is upset Steve Bennett awarded Liverpool a penalty in Sheffield United's 4-0 defeat

Ref Justice

"I don't think I'll comment further – last season it cost me a £2,000 fine from the FA. Then again, shall I read you what Carlos Queiroz said about one ref when he was with Man United? [Pulling out a piece of paper from his pocket]. He called the ref a 'disgrace' but he didn't get fined, did he?... I was upset at the end, definitely. For a start, I couldn't understand why the fourth official was busy shaking hands with the Birmingham bench while we were trying to send on our third substitute Johannes Ertl. I would have thought that was more important."

The Palace boss after Birmingham got a winner in the fourth minute of added time when three minutes was initially signalled

WAR OF WORDS

"I know when you get a chance lino, just try and show me you're not biased all the time, will ya!... Lino, he's kicked the f*cking ball out man! What the f*cking hell is happening?... F*cking top of the league, Premiership, they all get the f*cking decisions. With f*cking tosspots like that!... He should be f*cking flagging! Stuey, go and warm up down there and f*cking tell him he should be f*cking flagging for that, he's only 10 yards away from it... Fucking hey Joe! [Royle], that made my day complaining about him, f*cking hell Joe, come on'. He's [the ref] been your best f*cking player!... When you see that on telly tonight lino, and you see it's a penalty, would you feel disappointed or would you think 'I just made a mistake, it's alright'. You'll think, 'That'll teach Warnock!'"

A TV crew captures Warnock on the touchline

Ref Justice

"The officials were the worst team tonight. They were indecisive throughout and there was practically manslaughter on James Scowcroft."

The Palace boss after Leicester's late win

"For me, it's a vendetta by the fourth official to get me sent off and I don't accept it."

The Blades manager was sent to the stand after 'abuse' from the dugout against Leeds

"I think experienced referees should stay on but if Clive's [Penton] not fit enough to keep up with play there, that's not on."

Warnock takes a swipe at the man in black

WAR OF WORDS

"I wanted to make sure that we kept an eye on the offsides so I had my subs warming up with the linesman."

The manager gets his players to 'help' the assistant referee

"I don't comment on referees, never have done."

Warnock's view after Coventry's Micky Adams felt ref Colin Webster had been influenced by United's staff in sending off Matt Heath

"I think there might be one or two games where I don't get some decisions going for me – from people who have read my book!"

Warnock criticised refs in his autobiography

Ref Justice

"We've got Mike Riley, I've never been a big fan of his refereeing abilities. I've always thought Mike's done well on limited ability to get where he's got. He's what I call a robot referee and now he's in charge of our referees!"

The QPR boss slams the general manager of the Professional Game Match Officials

"He's an experienced referee, I feel really let down. I think the official has cost us, it was an absolute disgrace tonight. He said he didn't see Sol in the box. It's quite understandable, he is only 6ft 6in."

The Cardiff manager after Sol Bamba's late goal was controversially disallowed

WAR OF WORDS

"I think my half-time team talk did the trick really – I asked [referee Chris Foy] if he wanted some smelling salts, I didn't think the concentration level was good enough from him in the first half."

The Eagles manager offers the official a helping hand

"Fortunately, Graham Poll's retired so I won't have a problem from that point of view – there'll be no blame placed on him this time."

He reckons Palace can progress in the FA Cup but still hasn't forgiven Graham Poll over a big decision that cost Sheffield United against Arsenal in 2003

Ref Justice

"He's in England, isn't he? What do you expect? I suppose when you're like that you want everything to be nice and pretty but you don't get that in England."

The Cardiff boss on Pep Guardiola's complaints about aggressive tackles

"Mr Massey says if he's got it wrong he will be suspended for a couple of games. I said to him, 'When you're sat on your settee when you're suspended will you think about us?'"

Linesman Trevor Massey appeared to wrongly indicate a corner which led to Stiliyan Petrov scoring Villa's equaliser three minutes from time against Palace

WAR OF WORDS

"I thanked the referee for giving us three cracking throw-ins, even when one of them might have been their ball."

The Notts County boss is in good spirits

"I think that Peter Walton is one of the best referees in the country – and I'm not taking the p*ss. I bet you won't print that, you b*stards, will you, when it's something good?"

The Blades manager did have it printed

Printed in Great Britain
by Amazon